Jeremy Clarkson

The Original Petrol Head

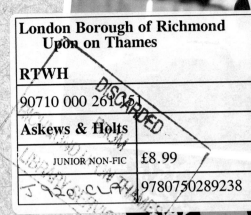

Published in paperback in 2016 by Wayland
Copyright © Wayland 2016

Wayland, an imprint of
Hachette Children's Group
Part of Hodder & Stoughton
Carmelite House
50 Victoria Embankment
London EC4Y 0DZ

Senior editor: Julia Adams
Produced for Wayland by Dynamo
Written by Hettie Bingham

PICTURE ACKNOWLEDGEMENTS:
Key: b=bottom, t=top, r= right, l=left, m=middle,
bgd=background

Alamy: p4 bl, p7 tl David J. Green; p25 tl Alamy Celebrity.
Corbis: p2 tr, p12 br Lotte/Splash News; p20 bl
Koen Van Weel/EPA. Getty: p4 m, p9 t, p11 m, p17 br, p17 br,
p17 br, p19 ml, p19 t, p 21 tl, p25 m; Getty Images Entertainment;
p8 br Photoshot; p16 bl AFP; p1 m, p5 tr, p15 tr, p24 mr, p14 bl,
p22 mr, p30 tr, p18 mr, p26 mr, p29 br, p30 tr Wireimage/Getty
Images. iStock: p16 EdStock. Shutterstock: Backgrounds and
doodles: Tracks Hugolacasse, MisterElements, Marie Nimrichterova,
LHF Graphis, Alexsandr Bryliaev, Aleks Melnik, PinkPueblo, mexrix,
topform, chronicler. p2 t Karen Roach; p5 tr featureflash, bl
EverenKalinbacak, br Keith bell; p6/7 Jiri Hira bgd, bl, p7 br Home
Studio; p8 br Georg Schmidt; p9 l vtls, b EverenKalinbacak; p10 br
Globe Turner, bm Stephania Hill, bm blackstroke, bl Paul Stringer; p12
t Kosarev Alexander, tr Fedor Selivanov, br Paul Stringer, bl Ravshan
Mirzaitov; p13 tl Fingerhut, tm Zoran Karapancev, mr foto76, mm
Gyuszko–Photo, ml Paul Stringer; p22 b Sean Nel, p23 tr Steffan
Foerester, b MR; p26 b robnroll, p27 t Gary Blakeley. Science Photo
Library: p7 tr NASA/Science Photo Library.

Dewey classification: 791.4'5'092-dc23

ISBN 978 0 7502 8923 8
Library E-book ISBN 978 0 7502 8560 5

Printed in China
10 9 8 7 6 5 4 3 2 1

An Hachette UK company
www.hachette.co.uk
www.hachettechildrens.co.uk

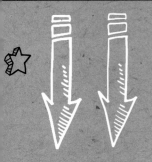

Jeremy Clarkson

JEREMY CLARKSON
The Original Petrol Head

■Jeremy is known for his outspoken opinions and tongue-in-cheek style. Sometimes he is criticized in the newspapers for the things he says, but he's not the type to be bothered by that! He is loved by many and others love to hate him, but few people are indifferent to his strong personality.

I bet you never knew this!

Jeremy's first job was selling Paddington Bear toys.

The Who

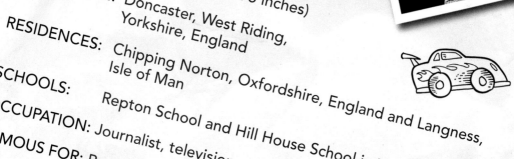

NAME: Jeremy Charles Robert Clarkson

BORN: 11 April 1960

HEIGHT: 1.96 metres (6 ft 5 inches)

HOMETOWN: Doncaster, West Riding, Yorkshire, England

RESIDENCES: Chipping Norton, Oxfordshire, England and Langness, Isle of Man

SCHOOLS: Repton School and Hill House School in Doncaster

OCCUPATION: Journalist, television presenter and author

FAMOUS FOR: Presenting Top Gear

LIKES: Cars, travelling, rock music (especially Genesis and The Who), engineering projects and military vehicles Oh yes, and cars!

JEREMY
Growing Up...and Up

POST OFFICE TELEGRAM

TELEGRAM 11.04.1960

ON MONDAY, 11 APRIL 1960, DONCASTER WELCOMED ITS NEWEST RESIDENT: JEREMY CHARLES ROBERT CLARKSON. HIS PROUD PARENTS WERE: EDWARD GRENVILLE CLARKSON AND SHIRLEY GABRIELLE WARD. A COUPLE OF YEARS LATER A LITTLE SISTER, JOANNA, CAME ALONG AND THE FAMILY WAS COMPLETE.

Growing up in a farmhouse in South Yorkshire, Jeremy had a happy childhood. Although never keen on school, he liked books – his favourite being the *Ladybird Book of Motorcars* from 1963.

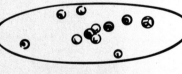

While Jeremy was busy dreaming of fast cars, his mother was busy building the family empire. She was a dab hand with a sewing machine and ran a business making and selling tea cosies. For Christmas 1971, Jeremy and his sister received a special present: their mum had made them Paddington Bear toys. Using fabric from the market, plastic eyes, a black button for the nose, wellington boots and a hat made of felt, the first Paddington Bears were born. Although none of them knew it at the time, this event was to change their lives. The toys were so admired by friends and neighbours that Jeremy's mum started to sell them through her business.

'The whole place was just one big bear factory.'

Shirley Clarkson, 2008

Shirley Clarkson didn't realize at first that she needed permission to make the bears. Michael Bond, who wrote the *Paddington Bear* books, got in touch to explain. They soon struck a deal that kept everyone happy. In fact, it was the beginning of a beautiful friendship and Jeremy's dad remained close friends with Michael Bond. Soon the Clarksons' old farmhouse became a bear-making factory. They had a pigsty which was converted into an office and they bought the local post office which became a design room.

When Jeremy was sixteen, he thought he was 'way too ugly ever to get a girlfriend' – but he hadn't reckoned on Paddington Power!

'I suddenly realized that Paddington was this huge draw... My mother designed Paddington Bear!'

Jeremy Clarkson, 2008

Jeremy in First Gear

Jeremy hasn't always been illuminated in the car headlights of fame. His first job wasn't at all glamorous... but it did involve a bit of driving.

When Jeremy was a young man of twenty one, he worked for the family business as a Paddington Bear salesman. This involved driving all over the country and taking orders. Although the Paddington toys were in great demand, Jeremy's mum once revealed that not all their salesmen were successful. Jeremy has joked that he won the 'Worst Salesman Ever' award in 1981.

The problem was that his heart just wasn't in it. He didn't like being in a hotel in the middle of a strange town and eating supper all by himself. He was worried that it looked as if he didn't have any friends.

I WAS UTTERLY RUBBISH.

WORST SALESMAN EVER

YES, YOU WERE BAD!

Jeremy's mother!

CLARKSON

Jeremy's career in sales didn't last long. He decided to become a journalist and trained with a local newspaper, the *Rotherham Advertiser*. He went on to write for other newspapers including the *Rochdale Observer*, *Wolverhampton Express and Star* and *Lincolnshire Life*. Jeremy had found something he was good at! He soon had an idea to combine his talent for writing with his love of motoring. In 1984 he set up the Motoring Press Agency (MPA).

Here he conducted road tests and wrote about them for local newspapers and car magazines. Before long he was writing for lots of different magazines. He still likes writing articles for car magazines and has had many pieces published in *Top Gear* magazine since its launch in 1993. He also writes articles and columns for national newspapers, *The Sun* and the *Sunday Times*.

The Top Gear Years

Top Gear is a television show featuring motoring and motor-sports. Being a presenter on this show is what Jeremy Clarkson is best-known for, but how did it all begin?

Top Gear was first broadcast in 1977, but it wasn't until 1988 that Jeremy Clarkson appeared on the show. It wasn't long before Top Gear became BBC Two's top-rated programme with more than five million viewers. Jeremy Clarkson left the show during the 1990s, and soon afterwards the viewing figures fell to below three million.

I bet you never knew this!

Australia, Russia, the USA and South Korea all make their own versions of Top Gear.

KEY DATES

Top Gear begins.	Jeremy Clarkson makes his first appearance.	The BBC stops broadcasting Top Gear.	The BBC launches a new-look Top Gear.
1977	1988	2001	2002

In 2001, the BBC stopped making *Top Gear* for a while but by 2002 it was back, with Jeremy Clarkson in the driving seat. Jeremy's co-presenters were Richard Hammond and Jason Dawe. James May replaced Jason after the first series.

The new show was recorded at Dunsfold Aerodrome in Surrey. It became known for its humour: the team often destroyed caravans and old cars, usually by dropping pianos on them!

The ex-*Top Gear* presenters proudly show off their award at the National Television Awards in 2007.

In 2015, the BBC announced that Jeremy, James and Richard would no longer be appearing in the show and presenter Chris Evans was confirmed as the new lead host.

JEREMY SAYS:

'SPEED HAS NEVER KILLED ANYONE. SUDDENLY BECOMING STATIONARY, THAT'S WHAT GETS YOU.'

Eight million people watch *Top Gear* – a record for BBC Two.

2007

Top Gear is voted programme of the decade by Channel 4.

2009

Jeremy leaves *Top Gear* and Chris Evans is confirmed as the new lead host.

2015

CARS CARS CARS

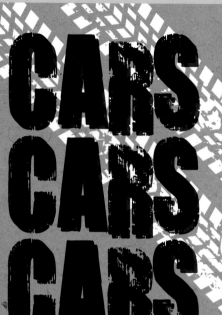

To say that Jeremy is rather fond of cars would be an understatement! Here are some of the cars that Jeremy has owned...

Aston Martin Virage

This grand tourer was manufactured between 1989 and 2000, and was the company's top model. Rumour has it that Mrs Clarkson likes to drive this one!

Lamborghini Gallardo

Lamborghini built ten thousand of these in the first seven years of production. It was their best-selling model.

Ford Escort RS Cosworth

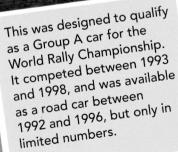

This was designed to qualify as a Group A car for the World Rally Championship. It competed between 1993 and 1998, and was available as a road car between 1992 and 1996, but only in limited numbers.

Ford GT

This was inspired by the 1960s racing car the Ford GT 40. Not many were imported to Britain, so Jeremy was lucky to get one. He wasn't happy with its performance though – it had lots of technical problems.

Mercedes-Benz SLK 55 AMG

Quick off the mark at 0-100km/h (62mph) in 4.9 seconds, this sports car is every petrol head's dream. Jeremy describes this type of car as sounding 'like the god of thunder gargling nails'.

I bet you never knew this!

Jeremy has destroyed twenty cars, including a Porsche 911, Maserati Biturbo and an Austin Allegro.

Lotus Elise 111S

This sports car is so light it can accelerate very quickly, even though its engine is not that powerful. Jeremy sent his Lotus back to have a sports exhaust fitted – the ordinary ones just weren't loud enough for him!

Mercedes-Benz SLS AMG

Launched at the 2009 Frankfurt motor show, this car is still in production. It is a front-engine, 2 seat, luxury grand tourer.

Honda CR-X

This was a front-wheel-drive sports compact car was produced between 1983 and 1991. It was marketed as an economy sports fastback, and has a top speed of 257km/h (160mph).

OUTSPOKEN CLARKSON

Jeremy is well-known for speaking his mind – whether on TV or in his newspaper column. Some people think he is rude and some think he is funny, but everyone would agree that he is never lost for words!

Jeremy's catch phrase:

‘ HOW HARD CAN IT BE? ’

Jeremy isn't keen on small cars. He once said:

'We all know that small cars are good for us, but so is cod liver oil!'

It is considered typically English to talk about the weather – we've probably all done it during an awkward silence. But Jeremy isn't happy with the way the forecasters tell us about it:

'Why is the forecast so bland? Why instead of "stormy" don't they just say the sea's a frothing maelstrom of terror and hopelessness?'

It would certainly be more entertaining that way!

'WE GET QUITE A LOT OF COMPLAINTS THAT WE DON'T FEATURE... AFFORDABLE CARS ON THE SHOW... SO WE'LL KICK OFF TONIGHT WITH THE CHEAPEST FERRARI OF THEM ALL!'

'USUALLY, A RANGE ROVER WOULD BE BEATEN AWAY FROM THE LIGHTS BY A DIESEL POWERED WHEELBARROW.'

Of course, we all know what Jeremy likes talking about most of all – cars! Here are a few of the cheeky things he's said on *Top Gear*:

'DURING THE BREAK WE GOT COMPLAINTS THAT WE DON'T SHOW ENOUGH GREEN CARS SO HERE'S ONE...' (pointing to a Lamborghini Murcielago ... in bright green.)

Grumpy Old Man

It was no surprise that Jeremy was full of grumbles when he appeared on the television show *Grumpy Old Men* in 2003. Here are some of the things he had to say …

On baby buggies:

'Pavements used to be big enough for two or three people to pass each other. Nowadays... I saw one of those prams the other day that had got double wheels on each side... a Range Rover doesn't need that – and it weighs nearly three tonnes!'

When newspapers can't make up their mind:

'Newspapers are full of stuff saying we've got a really big problem with the economy, everybody's living far too long and we're not going to be able to afford to keep old people. The next week: everybody's too fat, they're going to be dead at sixty – WHICH?!'

On nativity plays:

'All my children are always cast as something at the back. This year, I'm fully anticipating one of them to be the ears on the donkey!'

MILITARY INTERESTS

Jeremy has a keen interest in the British armed forces and military vehicles. This has often been reflected in his television shows.

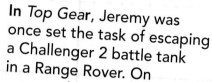

In *Top Gear*, Jeremy was once set the task of escaping a Challenger 2 battle tank in a Range Rover. On another occasion, a Lotus Exige sports car had to evade missile lock from an Apache helicopter. A platoon of Irish Guardsmen also appeared on the show to shoot at a Porsche Boxster and a Mercedes-Benz SLK. And if that isn't enough, a Ford Fiesta was used as a Royal Marine landing craft. In *Jeremy Clarkson's Extreme Machines*, a documentary series he made in 1998, Jeremy flew an F-15 military jet.

and HELP for HEROES

Jeremy's interest in the military is put to a good cause: he supports the charity Help for Heroes. He often attends events and visits homes for injured or retired military service personnel.

On a visit to Tedworth House recovery centre in Wiltshire, Jeremy joined some wounded soldiers to try out some three-wheeler handbikes. This was to promote a charity event called Hero Ride.

Jeremy said:

> It has been a very moving day today, visiting our heroes who have suffered life-changing injuries.

Jeremy's Military Tweets:

Just been to The Sun's military awards. All very humbling. Many great guys. Many great stories. Help a real hero today by downloading the new Help for Heroes game app!

Big congratulations to @UnsunkHeroes for Dragon Boat racing to raise money for @HelpforHeroes...

Just been for a curry with the Chelsea Pensioners. Met a man who actually helped build the Bridge on the River Kwai. Bit humbling.

Star Quality

Jeremy has bags of energy and enthusiasm. This, and his open and daring approach to everything he does, contribute to his star quality. His sense of humour has made him one of the most well-known and popular celebrities on television.

In 2007, Jeremy Clarkson won a 'Special Recognition Award' at the National Television Awards. This is an award that celebrates a unique contribution to television. He won the award as recognition for the part he played in transforming *Top Gear* from a 'niche show for enthusiasts into a must watch programme for millions of fans'. He was also noted for being a driving force behind highly acclaimed documentaries and historical profiles.

On accepting the award, Jeremy said:

> Thank you everybody for this – I don't know quite what to say; normally I prepare before I speak on television but I haven't had the chance because I didn't know this was going to happen.

Thanking his team he said:

> Top Gear is a team, well it's not a team really, it's a playground. It isn't work; it's just the most fun in the world.

The award was presented to Jeremy by racing driver Lewis Hamilton.

Lewis Hamilton

'IT GIVES ME GREAT PLEASURE... TO PRESENT THE SPECIAL RECOGNITION AWARD; GROWING UP, TOP GEAR WAS ALWAYS ONE OF MY FAVOURITE SHOWS AND IT STILL IS. I SHARE THE SAME PASSION AS JEREMY FOR CARS; THEIR SPEED, THEIR GRACE – AND HE'S ALWAYS GOT SOMETHING INTERESTING TO SAY. AND HE ALWAYS SEEMS TO MAKE ME LAUGH.'

Here's what his famous friends had to say about his Star Quality:

'HE SPEAKS HIS MIND.'

'WHAT THERE IS OF IT!'

'HE'S LIKE A 14-YEAR-OLD BOY TRAPPED IN A MAN'S BODY.'

'I THINK ONE OF THE CRUCIAL THINGS ABOUT JEREMY IS, HE IS DRIVEN BY THE STORY... AND HE DOES HAVE A REALLY ANNOYING HABIT OF REALLY CARING ABOUT WHAT HE'S DOING... WHEN YOU GET TOWARDS THE END OF A LONG DAY AND YOU THINK IT'S TIME TO GO HOME, HE TENDS TO THINK NO, NO, NO.'

Jimmy Carr

Jeremy's mum said:

His headmaster used to say to us that he'll either be very famous or he'll end up in jail... and I think I know what he meant.

(Jeremy has) always said there were two opinions; there's his and the wrong one.

ENGINEERING INTERESTS

Think of Jeremy Clarkson and the first subject that might spring to mind is cars. But did you know he has another interest that is maybe even stronger than motoring? Engineering is a subject very close to his heart.

When Jeremy appeared on the television programme *Who Do You Think You Are?* he revealed that most of the books in his house are about old machines. He has said that he is not good with his hands, but that doesn't mean he can't be fascinated by those who are.

The Industrial Revolution is of particular interest to Jeremy. He is a great admirer of these pioneering civil engineers:

⭐ **Isambard Kingdom Brunel,** the man who created the Great Western Railway, and designed many ships, tunnels and bridges.

⭐ **Thomas Telford** who designed tunnels, canals and bridges around the Shropshire area.

⭐ **Robert Stephenson** who invented an early steam locomotive called the Rocket or 'Stephenson's Rocket'.

I think it is engineering history that I like most of all.

In 2004, Jeremy presented a five-part documentary on BBC Two called *Inventions That Changed the World*. The five inventions that he covered in the series were:

THE GUN

According to Jeremy, the gun has had a 'bit of a chequered history'. On the up side, its invention has given us advanced trauma surgery (surgeons have had to learn new skills to treat gunshot wounds). On the downside it has killed lots of endangered species such as tigers (because people enjoy hunting as a sport).

THE TELEPHONE

Jeremy said that:

> We live in an invisible jungle of communication with millions of people talking to each other at any one time.

He thinks that most people would rather be without their trousers than without a telephone.

THE COMPUTER

'Without this invention we wouldn't be able to watch television, travel in space, fly a jet engine or talk on mobile phones,' Jeremy explained. All of these inventions use computer technology.

THE TELEVISION

'This changed the way information and entertainment could be conveyed to the masses. It was exploited by the Nazis in the Second World War when they used it to spread propaganda, but the very same thing helped us to win the war. It also helped to make us fat because people started to spend more time watching it and less time being active,' explained Jeremy.

> Quite simply, without it I wouldn't have a job!

THE JET

'When people first started flying in the 1960s, it was considered glamorous; people dressed up for it and there were no queues,' Jeremy pointed out. Now you have to spend hours queuing before you can get anywhere near the runway!'

Clarkson's Epic Car Journeys

I bet you never knew this!

Jeremy and James were the first people to reach the magnetic North Pole in a car.

Polar Expedition

In this ambitious expedition, the *Top Gear* presenters travelled from north Canada all the way to the North Pole – that's 724 kilometres (450 miles). Jeremy said he wanted to prove that 'Arctic exploration needn't be tough.' That was easy for him to say; while he and James travelled in an adapted pick-up truck, Richard had to rough it on a sled pulled by huskies. The journey presented many challenges, but Jeremy found a good solution to one of them: to avoid having to go to the toilet on the ice, he attached a toilet seat to his tow bar and named this new invention a 'bumper dumper'.

Botswana

The Makgadikgadi Pan is a large salt pan in the middle of the savanna in northeast Botswana. It was once an enormous lake, but it dried up thousands of years ago. The largest salt pan in the world, it is almost completely lifeless. Jeremy set out with his *Top Gear* pals to be the first people to cross it in a car.

Here's how Jeremy explained this mission to his mates

'If you run out of water you will die. If your car breaks down and you can't be rescued, you will die. If you run out of food, you will die. It's like driving on a 'crème brûlée'; there's primeval ooze covered with a thin layer of salty crust. If you have thin tyres, you will break through that crust, get stuck and you will die...'

South America

In 2009, the *Top Gear* hosts travelled 1,610 kilometres (1,000 miles) across South America. Starting out in the rainforests of Bolivia, they travelled all the way to the Pacific coast of Chile. Driving a battered Range Rover, Jeremy discovered the full horror of Bolivia's notorious Yungas Road or 'Death Road', as it is known. This road between La Paz and Coroico is very dangerous because it is narrow, winding and horribly dusty. The heart-stoppingly massive drops along the way have no safety barriers and would lead to certain death for any driver unfortunate enough to misjudge it.

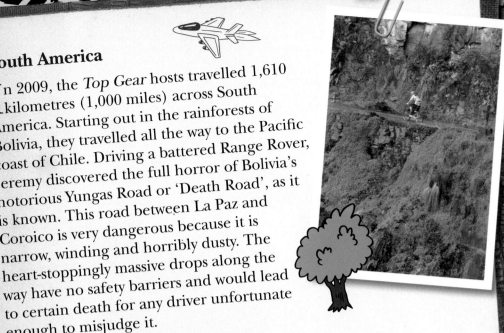

Vietnam

Ho Chi Minh City, which used to be named Saigon, is the largest city in Vietnam. It is from here that Jeremy set off on his 1,600 kilometre (1,000 mile) journey to Ha Long city in the north of the country. Jeremy and his mates made the journey on motorbikes this time.

JEREMY SAYS:

'RECENTLY, I SPENT EIGHT DAYS IN A CAR WITH MY CO-HOST FROM *TOP GEAR*, JAMES MAY, WHO HAS A NOTORIOUSLY FLATULENT BOTTOM. BUT BECAUSE HE WAS LIVING ON ARMY RATIONS THE INTERIOR WAS ALWAYS PINE FRESH AND LEMON ZESTY.'

Jeremy's other travel destinations include: Australia, Norway, the USA, Middle East, India and Africa.

FAMILY, FEUDS & FAMOUS FRIENDS

They say you should keep your friends close... and your enemies closer still!

Who are the people behind this famous petrol head? Jeremy Clarkson's first wife was Alex Hall. He was only married to her only briefly from 1989 until 1990. In 2010 Alex decided that she wanted to tell the world secrets about their relationship. Jeremy, however, decided that wouldn't be such a good idea and went to court to take out an injunction. This meant that, by law, she was not allowed to talk about it. The only problem with that was that the injunction itself was not a secret; it just made everyone curious about what Jeremy was trying to hide. So Jeremy lifted the injunction – and the things she had to say were perhaps not as interesting as all the things that people had been imagining!

Jeremy with his family at the *Mary Poppins* Gala Evening in London in 2005

When Jeremy got married again it was to Frances Cain in 1993. They have three children: Finlo, Emily and Katya.

Prince Harry meets Jeremy at a reception before the city salute pageant outside St Paul's Cathedral in London.

I bet you never knew this!

Jeremy passed his driving test in 1977 in his granddad's R Type Bentley. He was so sure that he would pass the test that he took some scissors with him to cut off the L-plates!

Jeremy's wife, Frances, is also his manager and has steered his career from the early days. Their family home is near Chipping Norton in Oxfordshire. They have been married for more than 20 years and some people have described Frances as his 'long suffering' wife. This is because Jeremy is so outspoken and always getting himself into trouble with what he says.

Piers Morgan

Jeremy has lots of famous and influential friends, including Prince Harry, but he has enemies too. One of Jeremy's most famous feuds is with the journalist, Piers Morgan. They have both said rude things about each other in public. When they were on the last ever flight of Concorde in 2003, Jeremy threw a glass of water over Piers. About a year later Jeremy punched Piers while they were attending the British Press Awards. More recently they have been having an argument on Twitter about whose television show gets more viewers.

Jeremy
ON THE
BOX

Jeremy is most famous for appearing on *Top Gear*, but there's more to this man than meets the eye. Not everything is about cars...

Robot Wars

In 1998, Jeremy presented the first series of *Robot Wars* with his co-presenter, Philippa Forrester. As the name suggests, this show was about Robots fighting each other. The robots were built by amateur mechanic enthusiasts who then entered them in fighting tournaments and friendly games.

Jeremy Clarkson Meets the Neighbours

In this 2002 series, Jeremy visited all the major European countries (our neighbours) to see if the reality matched our expectations. He drove off the ferry into France in an E Type Jaguar – a typically English car. He then explored the stereotypes that some English people apply to other nationalities to see if they were true. For example: that the French love garlic and are always chomping on frogs' legs.

The Victoria Cross: For Valour

In this programme from 2003, Jeremy looked into the history of the Victoria Cross, a medal awarded to soldiers for valour in the face of the enemy. It is the highest military decoration and was introduced by Queen Victoria in 1856. Only 1,357 medals have been awarded and of those, only 14 since the Second World War. Jeremy followed the story of one man who received the medal, Robert Henry Cain. At the end of the programme, Jeremy revealed that this man was his wife's father. She had no idea that her dad had received this very special medal until after he died.

Jeremy Clarkson: The Greatest Raid of All Time

For some time, Jeremy had been looking for another military story to follow on from his programme about the Victoria Cross, and in 2007 he found it. Known by military insiders as 'The Greatest Raid of All', this was a story little known by the general public. The operation he spoke of was a commando raid which took place during the Second World War. It was on a dry dock at St Nazaire in France, which was occupied by the Germans. The raid was so successful and heroic that five men were awarded the Victoria Cross as a result.

I bet you never knew this!

The Victoria Cross has always been manufactured by the London jewellers, Hancocks Ltd. The bronze it is made of comes from a melted down cannon which was captured from the Russians in the Crimean War (October 1853 – February 1856).

Are You Best Mates With...

JEREMY CLARKSON

By now you should know Jeremy like an old friend. Test your knowledge of him by answering these questions:

1 Which car did Jeremy receive as a Christmas present from his wife?
a) Noddy pedal car
b) Nissan Micra
c) Mercedes-Benz 600

2 Jeremy once worked as a salesman – what toy did he sell?
a) Sponge Bob Square Pants
b) Paddington Bear
c) Barbie

3 What type of vehicle did Jeremy drive on Bolivia's 'Death Road'?
a) Range Rover
b) Ford Fiesta
c) Lamborghini

4 Jeremy fashioned a special toilet device for his vehicle on his Polar Expedition – what name did he give to it?
a) The Jalopy Ploppy
b) The Bumper Dumper
c) The Pit Stop

5 How tall is Jeremy?
a) 1.96 metres
b) 3.2 metres
c) 1 metre

6 Which car does Jeremy say is a sensible family car?
a) Lotus Elise 111S
b) Aston Martin Virage
c) Volvo XC90

7 What are Jeremy's middle names?
a) Archibald Nelson
b) Charles Robert
c) Cosmo Ziggy

8 As a child, which role did Jeremy play in the BBC radio Children's Hour serial of the Jennings novels?
   a) Lord Snooty
   b) Just William
   c) Taplin

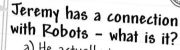

9 What lifted off from Cape Canaveral on the same day that Jeremy was born?
   a) Apollo 13
   b) The world's first weather satellite, Tiros I
   c) Superman

10 Jeremy has a connection with Robots – what is it?
   a) He actually is one
   b) He has a robot servant
   c) He presented the first series of Robot Wars in 1998

11 What is Jeremy's greatest interest apart from cars?
   a) Engineering
   b) Aliens
   c) One Direction

12 Which cute character does Jeremy think made him popular with the girls when he was sixteen?
   a) Mickey Mouse
   b) Shrek
   c) Paddington Bear

13 Who was Jeremy's co-presenter on Robot Wars?
   a) Philippa Forrester
   b) Jonathon Ross
   c) Richard Hammond

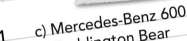

ANSWERS

1	c) Mercedes-Benz 600
2	b) Paddington Bear
3	a) Range Rover
4	b) The Bumper Dumper
5	a) 1.96 metres
6	c) Volvo XC90
7	b) Charles Robert
8	c) Taplin
9	b) The world's first weather satellite, Tiros 1
10	c) He presented the first series of Robot Wars in 1998
11	a) Engineering
12	c) Paddington Bear
13	a) Philippa Forrester

You can find more information about Jeremy Clarkson by:

logging onto the *Top Gear* website at www.topgear.com or following him on Twitter @JeremyClarkson.

Jeremy has written numerous books including five volumes of The World According to Clarkson:

Volume one – *The World According to Clarkson* (Penguin, 2005)

Volume two – *The World According to Clarkson: And Another Thing* (Penguin, 2007)

Volume three – *The World According to Clarkson: For Crying Out Loud!* (Penguin, 2009)

Volume four – *The World According to Clarkson: How Hard Can it Be?* (Penguin, 2011)

Volume five – *The World According to Clarkson: Is It Really Too Much to Ask?* (Penguin, 2013)

Other titles by Clarkson include:

Driven to Distraction (Penguin, 2010)

The Top Gear Years (Penguin, 2012)

GLOSSARY

Aerodrome
A place where flights take off and land, including cargo flights (not containing passengers)

Chequered history
A history or past with both good and bad parts

Crème brûlée
A custard-based pudding with a brittle, sugary crust

Crimean War
A war fought from October 1853 till February 1856 between Russia and an alliance of France, Britain and the Ottoman Empire

Dab hand
Particularly skilled

Flatulence
An excess of intestinal gas

Injunction
A court order that means a person, group of people or an organisation is made to stop doing something by law

Maelstrom
A very powerful whirlpool

Notorious
Famous for reasons that are not favourable

Pioneering
A person or people who explore a new area

Primeval
Belonging to the earliest age

Public-school
A school that charges parents a fee instead of receiving funding from the government

Tongue-in-cheek
Not entirely serious

Trauma surgery
An operation to repair very bad injuries

Understatement
A statement that could say more about something, but doesn't

Weather satellite
Equipment launched into space to orbit the Earth and monitor weather

Quote sources

Page 7 BBC Pebble Mill at One, 2008;
Page 8 BBC Pebble Mill at One, 2008;
Page 11 Top Gear, 2006; Page 14 Top Gear, 2008, Grumpy Old Men, 2003;
Page 15 Top Gear 2006-2009, Grumpy Old Men, 2003; Page 17 Twitter.com;
Page 18 National Television awards, 2007;
Page 19 National Television awards, 2007, Room 101, 2008; Page 20 Who Do You Think You Are? 2009; Page 21 Inventions That Changed the World, 2004; Page 22 Top Gear, 2007; Page 23 Top Gear, 2008

INDEX